To my kids.
You are my heart, you are
my life, you are my reason.

Nothing worth having is ever easy,
so never give up on your dreams!

Oggy Goes Shell Shopping

by Felicia Sais

illustrated by Mike Ferrin

Oggy the turtle lived in a shell, old and tattered, but it protected his back and that's all that really mattered.

After so many years of avoiding the change, Oggy's wife said he was stubborn. It was time for the exchange.

When he looked in the mirror, he knew
she was right. His damaged, dirty shell
was not a pretty sight!

It had cracks and holes from years of fun. He'd had so many adventures, and it had been with him through each one.

Oh, how he
feared that his
memories would
disappear! He
had the same
shell since he
was a hatchling
and had worn it
every year.

He'd played with his siblings, his cousins, and friends. Now, he was fifty and the shell's time had to end.

So Oggy called his best friend, a turtle named Rand. He needed some help for the hard task at hand.

Rand had gotten new shells since the two
had known each other, so he seemed the
perfect friend to help Oggy pick another.

The shells at the store had so many designs. They were covered in fresh coats of paint, and WOW, did they shine!

The shells had boosters, spikes, unique shapes and more. With so many options, they might never leave the giant store.

After hours of looking and trying some on, it was soon 7:30. Where had the time gone?

Just when he lost all hope of finding the right shell, Oggy saw something in the corner of his eye. Right away, he could tell.

It was a simple shell, and the paint job looked so clean. It was nearly all black with speckles of lime green.

There were no fancy gadgets, no pictures painted on top. But it fit Oggy perfectly and he felt as attractive as a beautiful swan.

Rand and Oggy checked out, and they walked home through the night. His wife beamed when he walked in. "I knew you'd find one that's just right!"

His old shell, he realized didn't fit like before. He really had loved that old shell, but he liked the new one even more.

Oggy learned there was no reason to fear what was new. He got a new shell, but kept his old memories too.

The end.

www.ingramcontent.com/pod-product-compliance
Lightning Source LLC
Chambersburg PA
CBHW040230070426

42448CB00033B/264